<u>Not Mine, Not Yours, But Ours</u>

How to reach financial unity in your marriage, and together build the
life you've always wanted.

By José R. Figueroa
Personal Finance Coach & Blogger @ Figueroa Financial

Not Mine, Not Yours, But Ours

Dedication

To my mom, Taty Santiago who encouraged me to seek and love God, to always do my best, to stay humble, and to be generous towards others. Love you mom!

Contents

Chapter 1: Introduction

Would you like to improve the odds of *success* for your marriage? I am sure the answer to this question would be a resounding *yes* whether you are engaged, newlywed, or you have been married for a while now.

Achieving success in your marriage has a lot to do with how well you are *coming together*, how well you are doing in achieving your marriage vows of building a new life by joining two separate lives.

When you think about it, it is a daunting task. You have two individuals with different backgrounds, family histories, preferences, views of the world, etc. Yet, we are told that we are to become "*as one*". I remember a preacher once saying the difficulty lies in the fact that there are days we don't even like ourselves too much, let alone another person.

After being married for a little over **10** years, I know that there are several dimensions to reaching unity in your marriage. I want to help you with an area which I believe will help you build a strong foundation for your life together.

In this book, I want to focus on how you and your spouse can reach *unity in financial matters*. Unfortunately, divorce statistics are still pretty high in the U.S. and financial/money problems are still one of the top causes for divorce.

You need to know that the only way to win with your money is to *work together with your spouse*. There is no other option. Healthy finances lead to healthy marriages.

When my wife and I came together on our finances, it strengthened other areas of our marriage, and it brought us to a new level of communication and intimacy. I know this can happen for you as well.

If we learn to work together with our money, we can put a dent in the divorce epidemic in our country. You and your spouse can build the life you've always wanted together.

Let's get started!!!

For this reason a man shall leave his father and his mother, and be joined to his wife; and they shall become one flesh.
Genesis 2:24 (NASB)

Chapter 2: How is your Financial Health?

In order to get to any destination, you first need to determine your starting point. Large buildings have directories with a red dot or a red X next to the words "**You are here**".

Before we can reach financial unity in our marriage, we need to start by determining where we are. To that end, I have created a short quiz to help you assess where you are as a couple.

It will only take a few minutes to complete. Scoring instructions and recommendations follow at the end of this chapter.

Let's figure out the *financial health* of your relationship:

1. You and your spouse have a standing meeting to discuss your household budget for the month before the month begins.

- Yes. We allocate every dollar to a spending category. (5 Points)
- Yes, but we keep it very high level, focusing only on the major categories. (3 Points)
- Not every month. We get busy sometimes and it gets away from us. (1 Point)
- We don't have a budget. All the money comes in and goes out, with no idea where it went. (0 Points)

2. You and your spouse make financial decisions together.

- Yes. Every purchase is discussed and prioritized as part of the monthly budget review. (5 Points)
- Not all of them. We have set a dollar figure up to which we each can spend without consulting the other person. (3 Points)
- A few. There are some I like to keep hidden. (1 Point)
- No. We each buy what we think is necessary without consulting with the other spouse. (0 Points)

3. You and your spouse have combined your finances.

- Yes. We have combined checking/savings accounts and we both know the all details about our finances. (5 Points)
- Partially. We have one checking account to pay bills but we also each keep separate checking accounts for our own expenses. (3 Points)
- No. We each keep separate checking accounts and we have split the bills. The rest we spend as we each see fit. (1 Point)
- No. You never know what's going to happen and I would like to keep my options open and my money safe. (0 Points)

4. You and your spouse have an equal vote when it comes to your money.

- Yes. We both have a say in the financial decisions. (5 Points)
- Yes, on the day to day expenses. However, since my spouse is better with finances, I just trust him/her with planning for retirement/college savings or the mortgage. (3 points)
- No. I am simply given an amount I can spend on certain categories. (1 Point)
- No. We never talk about money. It only leads to fights. (0 Points)

5. You and your spouse have agreement about your long term financial goals.

- Yes. We have a plan that we both understand and that we are both following. (5 Points)
- More or less. We agree on paying down the debt. But I would rather focus on paying the house first and my spouse is focused on saving for retirement first. (3 Points)
- No. We are having trouble agreeing on short term goals. (1 Point)
- No. We don't even know where to start on planning for the long term. We just hope it works out. (0 Points)

Now, let's add up your scores for the **5** questions:

1) Standing Budget Meeting: _____

2) Combined Finances: _____

3) Joint Financial Decisions: _____

4) Equal Vote in Money Matters: _____

5) Agreement on Long Term Goals: _____

Total # of Points: _____

Here is the scoring scale:

- **20-25 Points:** You and your spouse have a very healthy relationship when it comes to money and you are on your way to financial wellness.

- **15-19 Points:** You are having some of the right conversations but you need to come together on all aspects that relate to your money.

- **10-14 Points:** You are acting more like a joint venture instead of a unified household. You need to join forces together right away.

- **0-9 Points:** You are totally working independently of each other and you need to get some help today to get your finances in order.

So how did you do? If you scored above **15** points you are doing pretty well, but you can do better. If you scored less than **15** points you need more help but you should not be discouraged. That's why I wrote this book!

If you are not working with each other, you are working against each other. In order to win with your finances you have to be *honest* with each other, *patient* with each other, and you have to *work* with each other.

There is no other way to win with your money. You need each other. And I want to help you and your spouse to work as one on your money.

Let's see how we can help you improve your financial health!

[9] Two are better than one because they have a good return for their labor.
[10] For if either of them falls, the one will lift up his companion. But woe to the one who falls when there is not another to lift him up.
Ecclesiastes 4:9-10 (NASB)

Chapter 3: The 3 Foundational Stones for Financial Unity

Coming together on your finances will give you a good foundation as you embark on the great adventure of building a life together. But how can we get there?

What are the critical elements in reaching that level of unity? Every building that is designed to last, is built on a strong *foundation*.

Even the Bible speaks to the idea of a "*cornerstone*" and the idea of building your life on the "*rock*".

Here are the *3 foundational stones* to reach financial unity with your spouse: *Communication*, *Planning*, and *Execution*.

Communication

You need to be *open and honest* with each other in the area of finances. Talk about your dreams and your goals as well as your fears. Discuss the mistakes you have made previously with money.

We *all have made mistakes with money*, but the important thing is to know what we learned from those mistakes so we don't repeat them again.

Talk about what you know, and things you'd like to understand better such as investing, insurance or real estate. In your conversations, talk about how your respective families handled money, because that will have an effect on your own view of handling money.

Your pronouns need to change from *"you"* and *me"* to *"we"* and from *"yours"* and *"mine"* to *"ours"*. This applies to both income and any debt obligations. One combined income, one combined set of assets and liabilities.

There is no longer just one of you, but two people working to become one.

Remember, if you don't work with each other, you will be working against each other.

Planning

Now that you have all the proverbial cards on the table, you need to **develop a plan** to get your finances under control. There is a great deal of information available today.

You could read a book on personal finance. On my website you can find a list of books I recommend in this area:

http://www.figueroafinancial.com/recommended-reading/

Another way to get new information is to take a class together such as Dave Ramsey's Financial Peace University (FPU) or training available from Crown Financial Ministries.

Finally, you could also get personalized help from a financial coach who can give you objective, specific recommendations for your situation.

The point is, you need new information and new tools to help you go where you need to go.

A **good financial management plan**, will include a monthly budget, savings for emergencies, and paying down on debt. There are other elements, but first and foremost the plan should enable you to get control of your money.

If you don't manage your money well, the lack of management will be your downfall.

Execution

This is the hardest part of your journey. You can decide to finally talk about money and you can get all kinds of great information to put a great plan on paper. But you have to execute the plan!

Your **degree of commitment to execution** is what will determine your level of success. In order to fuel that commitment, you need to have both short long term goals in mind.

For example, a short term goal is finishing your emergency fund or paying off the next debt on your list. You could also have the short term goal of saving for a quick vacation. Long term goals could include saving for a car replacement or a down payment for a house.

In either case, goals will help you focus your efforts. Having control of your money, building up savings, eliminating debt will give you options you don't have today.

With your finances under control you could start dreaming again. Your marriage could **reach a new level of unity** you did not know was possible.

You could really change the financial destiny of your family for generations to come. You could give and help others like never before.

Change can be difficult, but sometimes it is absolutely necessary. There will be a price to pay to go from where you are today to where you want to go tomorrow. There is **no victory without sacrifice**.

Only you can decide to pay that price. **Is it worth it to you**? Is the success of your marriage and the destiny of your family important enough for you to change your ways?

"Marriages are not static. You are either pulling each other closer or the world is pulling you apart."
Mike Glenn

Chapter 4: Why You Should Combine Your Finances

When it comes to money management, one of the most common questions for married couples is: ***should we combine our finances?***

In my opinion, the short answer is ***yes***. Of course, there might be an extreme situation where addictive behavior (e.g., drugs/alcohol/gambling) makes the combining of finances unwise.

Trust is easily broken, and in order to take the step to combine your money, you need to be able to trust each other.

In general however, the best approach for a couple is to handle their money together (if you are engaged, wait until after you are married).

And here is ***why you should combine your finances***:

Transparency

Everything is on the table and all of the financial details are known to both of you. What are the assets we own? How much money comes in every month? How much money is owed and to whom? What are our monthly bills?

There are ***no secrets*** and because of that there are ***no surprises***. This transparency allows you to build the trust that is essential for both of you to win with money (Proverbs 27:23).

Teamwork

When ***both*** of you know the details of your finances, you both can contribute to the decisions that need to be made. You both have the information so you both can help with the day to day management of money.

Each of you has an equal vote and no one person is left carrying the emotional load by themselves. Two is indeed better than one (Ecclesiastes 4:9).

Terminology

In a marriage, we are supposed to be moving towards oneness (Genesis 2:24). This also applies to our money, so we need a new language to deal with finances.

When you combine your finances you are putting into action the change in your ***terminology*** regarding your money.

You can no longer refer to something as "***yours***" or "***mine***". You may have brought student loan debt to the marriage, but now, both of you have student loan debt.

One spouse might have run up debt on credit cards, but now both of you have credit card debt that needs to be paid off.

Only one of you may be an income earner, but all the money that comes in for the household is "***our money***". One spouse makes more money than the other. **Both** spouses have an *equal* say in money matters.

Money management can be very challenging. As a couple, you could make it extra hard on yourselves if you are pulling in different directions.

Put your marriage vows into action and decide that you will combine your finances. It will be the clearest indicator that you are indeed building a life together, for better or for worse.

> *"Many marriages would be better if the husband and the wife clearly understood that they are on the same side."*
> *Zig Ziglar*

Chapter 5: How to Agree on Major Purchases

As you get your budget under control, get out of debt, and build an emergency reserve, you will have increased cash flow.

And with more money coming in, you will have the opportunity to make **major purchases**.

The question is, how do you decide on what to purchase first? Let's assume of course that you will save the money for the expense and will not use debt. How then do we agree on a **priority order** on the purchases?

Invariably, you and your spouse will have different ideas on what to buy. One of you may want to save the money for a nice vacation while the other person wants to beef up the emergency reserve a little more.

Or one of you wants to do a home remodeling project that has been put off for a while, and the other person wants to buy a full entertainment system.

Here is an approach my wife and I have used in the past to come to an agreement about large purchases. As you look at your shared goals, this simple process might help you as well:

- Make a **list** of all the potential expenses. Examples include: vacation, car replacement, kitchen remodel, new couch, big screen TV.

- Determine an **estimated cost** to each item.

- Each person then goes down the list and assigns a **priority** (e.g, 1 to 10) to each item.

- Compare your priorities. **Share with each other** why each item is important.

- Come up with a combined priority list. Here is where the *art of compromise* comes in. Remember that you are building a *life together*, so surely you can *build a priority list together*.

- Total the amount required for all items. Based on your financial picture you might not get to all of them this coming year. But you will get to the items that are important to both of you.

This simple approach will let you know where to target your savings and you have a *common set of goals*. This is better, because sooner or later, you both get to win, you both get what you want.

> [3] *Do nothing from selfishness or empty conceit, but with humility of mind regard one another as more important than yourselves;* [4] *do not merely look out for your own personal interests, but also for the interests of others.*
> *Philippians 2:3-4 (NASB)*

Chapter 6: Develop a Financial Management System

When you decide to work together with your spouse on your finances, you are demonstrating:

- ***Respect for your Spouse***. You are saying that you respect your spouse's capability and intellect to handle money.

- ***Trust in your Spouse***. You are saying that you know they have integrity and honesty and can be trusted with money matters.

- ***Humility before your Spouse***. You are honestly acknowledging you don't know everything and that you can use some help in dealing with your finances.

When you deal with your spouse with respect, trust, and humility in the management of your finances, you will reach a new level of ***intimacy*** in your relationship.

What's the practical side of working together on your finances? In order to handle your finances well, you need to develop a ***financial management system***.

And the best way to demonstrate respect, trust, and humility with our spouses is to have a system where both you have ***equal access*** to the information and ***equal ability*** to handle and act on the information.

Now, it is quite possible that one of the spouses routinely handles most of the load of managing the finances (e.g., preparing the budget, paying the bills, etc.). But what happens if that spouse is not available for an extended period of time?

This situation could be due to an illness, being away from the home for work or family matters, or in the worst possible scenario, that spouse dies. What happens then? Can the other spouse pick-up the load?

Again, both spouses need ***access*** to all the financial information and the ***ability*** to ***act*** on that information.

Here are the key elements of your *financial management system*:

1. How Do We Pay the Monthly Bills?

Your *monthly budget* should tell you where the money is going before the month begins. However, both you and your spouse need to also know the following with respect to your monthly expenses:

- What are our monthly bills?

- When are the payments due for each bill and when are the payments made for each bill?

- What is the name and contact information for the payees for each bill?

- How are the payments made (e.g., paid through your on-line banking system, regular check via mail, etc.)

- How are we tracking monthly expenses?

It does not matter if your bill payment system is the old fashioned checkbook register, an Excel spreadsheet, a software program like Quicken, or an on-line program like Mint.com or YNAB.

It does not matter if it is a combination of some of these tools; the point is that both spouses need the *access* and the *ability* to use the system to pay your monthly bills.

2. What are Our Assets and Liabilities?

Besides being able to handle the monthly bills, both spouses need the ability to access the information on all your *assets (what you own)* and *liabilities (what you owe)*. You both need to be able to ascertain what your *current financial position* is at all times.

Assets

You need the documentation on each of these *asset accounts* listed below. If there is paper documentation make sure you both know where it is stored.

But also, in today's world, much of this information is kept on-line, so make sure you both know where to go get the information and how to access it (provider's web sites, user ids, passwords, account numbers, etc.).

You both should be able to access all the details and statements on the following:

- Checking and Savings Accounts

- Investment Accounts

- Retirement Accounts

- Medical Savings Accounts (e.g., Health Savings Accounts (HSAs), Flexible Spending Accounts (FSAs))

- Home Appraisals

Liabilities

It is very important that you know what your *financial responsibilities* are at all times.

Again, much of the information today is kept on-line so you both need the access information. But if you also have a physical filing system, make sure you both know where it is kept.

You need to know what the current balances are as well as the record of payments made.

- Credit Cards

- Car Loans

- Student Loans

- Personal Loans

- Medical Bills

- Mortgage Statements

3. Where are our Key Household/Estate Documents?

Finally, both spouses should be able to access these *key household/estate documents* at all times. Some examples of these documents are:

- Deed/Title information on your personal home and any other real estate you own.

- Insurance Policies (Life/Auto/Health/Home/ID Theft/Long Term Disability/Long Term Care)

- Tax Returns

- Credit Reports

- Wills/Trusts

Regardless of how you implement it, your household needs a financial management system. And if you are married, both spouses should have the ability to access and act on that management system.

Take sometime today to make sure you *love each other well* by taking the step to create or revise your system.

"God designed marriage to be a blessing. He intends married couples to use money — even challenges with money— to bring them closer together rather than separating them."
Howard Dayton

Chapter 7: A Final Word to the Husbands

I wanted to say a final word to my fellow men in this last chapter in the way of a challenge and an encouragement.

If you are married, you are in the leadership role already by God's design. If you are single, you need to learn to take control of your finances now so you can lead your wife and family later on.

Do you remember a series of commercials a while back asking us to "*man-up*"? Well, it's time to man-up about our money.

To help us with our discussion I would like to use the following Bible verse which speaks to the way men should act:

> *13 Be on the alert, stand firm in the faith, act like men, be strong.*
> *14 Let all that you do be done in love.*
> *I Corinthians 16:13-14 (NASB)*

What does "*acting like men*" mean when we talk about our finances? Let's unpack this verse and see how it could be applied to help us achieve manly money management. There are 4 things you and I need to do:

1. Be on the Alert

Some other translations indicate to "be on guard" or "to be watchful". When it comes to your money, how well are you keeping track of it? Do you balance your checkbook every month?

Do you keep track of your expenses? Do you plan how the money will be spent ahead of time? Do you have a good understanding of your investments?

You need to pay attention to what happens with your money. (Proverbs 27:23).

2. Stand firm in the Faith

The idea here is stand firm in what you believe, in the Word of God, the sure foundation of life.

The Bible has a lot to say about money and possessions. In His Word, God has laid out the best way to manage the money He has entrusted to us.

You and I would be foolish to ignore His advice (I Chronicles 29:11, 14-16).

3. Act like men, be Strong

Men are supposed to take the leadership role at home. This means *you lead the discussion* on money as well. Where is your family going? What are your goals?

You can't abandon your wife financially by leaving her alone with the burden of managing your finances. You have to be actively involved. And guess what: if there is a need to work extra hours or take a second job, you are up.

You *take the lead in making the necessary sacrifices*. It is your job to make sure your family is well taken care of financially (I Timothy 5:8).

4. Let all that you do be done in Love

Even though you are in the lead that *does not make you a dictator*. Your wife has an equal vote. Remember that you need to work together on your money, make decisions together.

Love your family well by saving for emergencies, retirement, and college. Finally, love your family well by taking care of what happens after you are gone. Make sure you have the proper level of life insurance and that you complete a will.

Love them to the end (I Corinthians 13:4-7).

What do you think? We men can get worked up about a lot of things in life that have no bearing on the destiny of our family. We can get really excited about our toys (cars, electronics, and man caves) and watching our sports.

But what if we were at least half as passionate about what happens with our finances and our families? Imagine that for a moment. Are you ready to man-up with your finances? Are you ready for manly money management?

"What higher motive could there be for the husband to love his wife? By loving her as Christ loved the church, he honors Christ in the most direct and graphic way.

He becomes the embodiment of Christ's love to his own wife, a living example to the rest of his family, a channel of blessing to his entire household, and a powerful testimony to a watching world."
John MacArthur

Appendix A. About the Author

José Figueroa was born and raised in Puerto Rico but has been living in the Lone Star State of Texas for over **22** years. After spending time in Houston and Austin, he is now living in Frisco, just north of Dallas.

He has a passion for helping people *get control of their money*. José understands from personal experience that managing finances can be challenging and overwhelming.

José married his wife Stacey in March of 2003. They are members of Prestonwood Baptist Church in Plano. They have one grown son (Brent Jett) who works as a Graphic Designer in Austin, TX.

<u>**Contact Information:**</u> You can reach José via any of the following methods:

- Website: www.figueroafinancial.com
- e-mail: jose.figueroa310@gmail.com

Connect Via Social Media

Facebook: www.facebook.com/figueroafinancial

Twitter: https://twitter.com/FigueroaFin

LinkedIn: http://www.linkedin.com/in/jrfigueroa

Google+: https://plus.google.com/u/0/b/111459341392513036380/111459341392513036380/posts

Pinterest: http://pinterest.com/jfigueroa310/financial-coaching/

www.ingramcontent.com/pod-product-compliance
Lightning Source LLC
Chambersburg PA
CBHW071605170526
45166CB00004B/1803